IF WE COULD KNOW OUR BONES

Two words--"listen; build"--nest quietly in one of the poems from Mary Carroll-Hackett's beautiful/tough/fragile collection, *If We Could Know Our Bones*. They are seeds from which she conjures and nurtures a world of words simple and complex; lives brief and infinite; love physical and soul-full; spirit deeply rooted in the earth and carried on the wind. "The apples don't last. She buys them anyway," she writes, and: "The only reason to live / is to give ourselves away." We do... to her poems... without hesitation--Robert Gray, Editor, *Shelf Awareness*

The wisdom in Mary Carroll-Hackett's *If We Could Know Our Bones* spans the width of the universe springing from a moment in time. It spans time from its elemental beginnings to a contemporary couple bound in each other's arms and legs as it has been since the beginning. She weaves the science of understanding and the magic of everyday living. We stand in wonder at the miracle and intimacy of nourishment and take sweet flight into the unknown and intuitive. These gems cut from words are earthy and heavenly, transcendent and rooted in the dirt of our becoming and our reckoning. These prose poems offer us shelter and meaning in the everyday, yet reach out to brush the hair back out of the face of the immortal as if to say, "God, let me see your eyes." Intimate and strange they occupy a place thumping within the physical human heart and the other heart we cannot fathom. Read this book, friends, not for answers, but to have the birdshot of goose bumps pepper your flesh on a summer day and wonder at the shared breath you take now from the one taken by ancestors long dead. Reading *If We Could Know Our Bones* is like knowing the science of why you have goose bumps. Mary Carroll-Hackett gives us concrete wonder like no other I know.

Jerry D. Mathes II, author of *Ahead of the Flaming Front: A Life on Fire* and *Fever and Guts: A Symphony*.

IF WE COULD KNOW OUR BONES

Mary Carroll-Hackett

© A-Minor Press
http://aminorpress.com/

for

Yonah Usdi

John Little Bear Eaton

always

Acknowledgments

Some of the poems here were originally published in the following journals. Thanks to these editors for their encouragement and for their continuing efforts toward the beautiful work, the good and too often thankless work for literature and art and heart that so benefits us all.

Special thanks to Slipstream Press and Katywompus Press for the chapbooks in which some of these poems appeared: *The Real Politics of Lipstick* and *Animal Soul*, respectively.

The Prose-Poem Project
Drunken Boat
Superstition Review
Apostrophe
Mindkites
Doorknobs & Body Paint
Buffalo Creek Review
Pedestal Magazine
SNReview
Third Wednesday
The Potomac
Procreation
MindKites
Praxilla
Alimentum
Stone's Throw Magazine
Steam Ticket
Blood Lotus
Epiphany
Cactus Heart
Dove Tales

Cover Picture: Eryk Wenziak
Design & layout: Walter Bjorkman

Copyright: ©2014 Mary Carroll-Hackett

ISBN: 978-0615933610 (A-Minor Press)

First Edition, A-Minor Press

Table of Contents

Book of Beginnings	15
The Dove Came First	16
Conjugation	17
The Man Who Wanted to See	18
Anthropology	19
Grave 43	20
Paper at the End of Century	21
Remembering the Body as Grace	22
The Lesser Prophet	24
Stockings	25
She	26
Neanderthal	27
What He Said About a Dancer's Body	28
At Caddo	29
Personal Genomics	30
Announcement	31
We Stood with You	32
Bear Watches from the Woods	33
If We Could Know Our Bones	34
Synesthesia	35
Dimes	36
This Bread, Those Beans	37
The Food She Makes Him	38
On Not Being Carried	39
Marooned	42
He	43
Bread	44
In the Jungle You Discover	45
When My Dead Father Comes to Visit	46
The Dove That Calls	48
Placing	49
Words Like River, November	51

Writ During War	52
Funeral Food	53
Upon Waking I Remember	54
Catfish	55
Encounter with Realism as a Child	56
Six Rules For Devils	57
What Took Root	58
Women Now and the Trick of Avoiding Touch	59
This Picture of Himself	60
Bad Moon	61
That Mother in Gaza	62
After the Owl at Chavet, Taino	63
When the Dark Comes	64
To Water, From Water	65
Talking in Tongues	66
It	67
The Marine at the Bowling Alley	68
The Man at the Party	70
Galileo's Fingers	71
Showing Nightly	72
Bestia Animus	73
We All Need Those Forty Days	74
It is as One Body	75
The Real Politics of Lipstick	76
Why She Keeps Leaving	77
We Buried the Arrows	78
Sitting Naked in the Yard	79

IF WE COULD KNOW OUR BONES

In the Book of Beginnings

my belly stretched brown and round, taut and humming beneath your warrior hands, the squared ends of your fingers naming, claiming a thousand children's tiny bones, feet like wings, fluttering beneath my ribs, swimming toward the sacrum. I slept fitfully between your knees. Beyond us, above the mountains, the drumming grew louder. There in the fields, three lions, blue-gray and gentle—for now—waited in the soft grass, murmuring *take the children to the trees*. In the flicker of your lamps, I lifted the robes, so I could show you what we'd made together, the gates and spirals tattooed there, loops burned into the skin above my left hip, guarding against loss of what grew within, schemata for that future we were seeding. *Don't cry for me, Magdalena.* You spun me into beginning again, a voice in the wind, in my hair, leading me to that day when the hawks would cross into view, serpentine clawing open the stark sky, for that day when the leonine eyes would widen to orbs, allowing all that is light in.

The Dove Came First

to eat the seed I spread, wing soft as ash, gray glow, white chest, against the grass your grandmother planted most of a century ago. Through the open window, I hear you breathing.

I will not speak of leaving, refuse the idea of plans, so you buy more bags of corn, for me, for my cousins the birds, sugared kernels in the cup of your hands, as you patiently show me new the limits of words, their lettered bones brittle, useless with want against a sky that old. I fold your fingers into mine, and listen, without talking—for once.

We are east and west, the medicine says, points in compass balance, kneeling, leaning into each other at last, across plates of potatoes and beans, the hanging of curtains, teeth in a glass, the interrupted sleep of loving bodies half a century old. I fret—children, gardens, the pull and mourn of worry that keeps me touching you—you say, come here, girl, and in your arms, I sleep, while you whisper, rest, rest, it will keep.

Conjugation

Fourth person tense, this sliding of food into your mouth, a bite of bread, ground, oiled and herbed, I worry—about the prick of rosemary needles on your tongue, what's said when the sand won't shake from my fingers. I worry the beads at my throat—*audiō, muniō, audīre, munīre, audīvī, munīvī, audītus, munītus*—listen; build. They quake like birds, click like talons, conjugations my father taught us and words worried—*sciturus*—to know, future perfect, this Latin tense looking at both ends of an action, the loaf folded over on itself, rising most historically, excessively, in the Gospel of John, less accident than evaluation, deliberate by the evangelist, who worried, convinced that the effect was still as abiding, that fourth person still known—*sentiō, sentīre, sēnsī, sēnsus*—perceived, retrieved now, here, in the bread we made, the oil ripe and slick as Jerusalem olives, the rosemary worrying us to remember, remember.

The Man Who Wanted to See

Phoenicians cooking over sand discovered glass, but it would be five thousand years before glass curved to lens, before a spectacle maker, standing late at a bench, repairing reading specs for the wigged banker, glanced up as one loose lens tumbled across his work table. He held it between square fingers, turned it with care until it caught and shone, a pull of what might be seen, a tug to the yellow blur of the lamp, his work forgotten, as he spun the lens until the thought of light broke in his hand, like a star, like the sun. Thoughts of the sun moved him to the window, even while the night held tight outside, even while his wife turned heavily in their iron bed, her breath a rhythm around him, and he pushed open the window, the lens drawn out into the air, raised to the sky and in the quiet, he stood squinting, squinting, dreaming space into, becoming, in that moment, the father of Galileo Galelei, his silent gaze splitting open the sky, revealing what we would see—craters on the moon, sunspots, the four large moons of Jupiter, the rings of Saturn, possibility of the universe—later. Even Galileo could see no more than a quarter of the moon's face without repositioning his telescope. But this night, this man, as his wife dreamed of the beans and bread she would offer for breakfast, and his son kicked loose a tussle of quilt on his small corner bed, his childish feet arched and white, this spectacle maker lifted a single curved mirror to gather in light, his quiet weary eye lifted toward the sky, looking, looking.

Anthropology

That thing she did, with her mouth, her tongue, she practiced in front of a mirror, because everyone knows it's all in the lips, all in the opening and closing, all in the need to lick, swallow, consume, devour. That man, he saw it, knew it, understood it, from the inside because he practiced too, the swagger, the suave, the lope, drawing her eyes to his thigh, to his legs, to the edges of the savannah where they'd known each other before, where they'd hunted and prowled and lingered by fires of their own making. Another epoch, another landscape, where shadows were predatory and lines were drawn with ragged sticks, where weapons were sharpened, for slicing secrets open, were blunt-edged, for bludgeoning, where bodies openly ached, craved, celebrated, where bodies were made for primal combat.

Grave 43

after Varna 4600-4200 BC

Developers, looking forward, not back, accidentally found him in 1972. Run up by an excavator, almost ground away beneath the cavernous bite of a backhoe, in a line of crouched and extended inhumations, in the company of two hundred ninety-four other burials. Some graves stood empty, bereft of bone, housing only cenotaphs, grave gifts, three thousand gold artifacts found all together. But Grave 43 shimmered, shook, holding more gold than has been found in the entire rest of the world for the epoch. Masks of unburnt clay looked on, accoutrements of power and wealth. This man mattered, had traveled, took with him the spoils, silver cup and painted bowl, of trade relations with distant lands, for which he paid with metal goods and salt copper ore, this primitive currency amassing him all that would prove his worth for lives to come. In his hand, a war adze, a mace at his side, a gold penis sheath strident between his thighs, bull-shaped gold platelets, record of his virility. Imagine that day, that bright Bulgarian sun, when he rose from between the thighs of his wife, packed extra dried meat, cheese and bread in his bag, something for those he might meet along his way to becoming a man worthy of being buried in Grave 43.

Paper at the End of the Century

She followed, point by point, the instructions on the hand-bill, the tri-folded paper shoved in the crook of her door at some point in the day while she had perched over her keyboard, entering names and numbers and places of dwelling for the hospital records. Driving home, she expected all to be the same on her street, 1101 Lilac Way, houses built on the same plan, only the never-paint-again siding varying in hue, hunched behind curbs neatly trimmed by the homeowner's association. Carefully, she removed the hand-bill from the regulation screen door, didn't read it until she had tucked her purse away, slid her shoes beside the bed— never under as that was a sign of impending death—and boiled water for tea. Then, having read, memorized actually, the instructions, she carefully, reverently, folded the paper in quarters, then in tens, then again in a thousand equal little squares. Her work completed, she went to bed for the night, sheets like an envelope, hands tucked in a tight little knot under her pillow. In the morning a man she'd never seen, didn't know, washed shamelessly in front of her mirror. As he shaved, she counted the strokes of blade against skin, razor rasping dangerously over bone on his unfamiliar jaw line, water droplets tangling, winking at her from the curls on his chest. She found her purse where she'd left it, then started a bit at her shoes shoved back under the bed. Kneeling to reach them, she looked up to see the man she didn't know but who had come at her request. He smiled at her reflection, and with a quiet finger drew a curlicue heart in the mist on the mirror. She looked around before she left the house, but the paper, creased and folded so many times, soiled by the touch of her fingers just yesterday, had disappeared.

Remembering the Body as Grace

for DE

We all live in a house on fire —*Tennessee Williams*

1

I dream back the hot slow sky your body was above me, goldleafed and dappled in early sun, in those running heated days of baggy shorts, thin shoulder straps, loosed barefoot in the woods, where the world wore the soft warm pelts we tumbled in, skins multicolored scarfs we slid out of, slid into, each other. We were hungering home.

2

I wore some long breezy skirt, thinking Stevie Nicks would approve; in those days music made our maps. At a party to honor the March stars, I sat in your lap on Alan's floor, after too much tequila, naming fish, aquarium after aquarium lining old apartment walls. Outside, a vernal moon split the day in two perfect halves, calling the first point of my Aries into startling alignment with your laugh.

3

Thirty-one suns have crossed the celestial equator since then, science and memory rearranging, the Earth's elliptical orbit, bending, changing, precession, axis tugged in another direction. Spring even now is being reduced by one minute per year, singing as it goes. Naked to the native acre, bone-clear, the body knows what it knows.

4

Age has freed us from any need to hide, that sweet surrender of knowing celestial objects near the celestial equator are visible worldwide.

5

Assuming the body as love, my body remembers—you sleepy-eyed and unshaven, hair long, lit by light breaking into that space, where we tangled like sweet-sweating animals. What we didn't know then, spring sliding home into summer, we do now, having worn these faces, lived in these skins, long enough to comprehend gravity as grace.

The Lesser Prophet

digs in his pockets for skeleton keys, for hands that know the feel of dough properly risen, for the words of prayers never to be learned in books, for the looks of tenderness only given, only possible, after half a century of living in this skin. He collects bags of coins, matchbooks, torn sheet music with songs about soldiers, singing as he walks the woods. He was a good soldier, a warrior once, and there among the hardwoods, away from the house, he comprehends the sharp edges of what it means to be ending. The neighbors come with pie because they know he's alone. He gives them flint in return, pieces of stone for sparking a flame because he wants to keep protecting them, because he knows how the cold and dark of night can burn.

Stockings

When my daughter was born, I vowed to give up wearing stockings, mesh torn from my knee-locked legs, I tied them in knots, cast them silky-limbed nets into the river.

Minnows flashed silver just beneath red-brown water.

The men I have dressed for, undressed for, all become fluid at some point, seed spilt deep between the joints of my hips, left me flailing, white eyes lined, lips blue, out of breath. The one whose tongue was the last piece of fruit in my mouth, peach I remember now, poet brooding into his shoes, face strung tight, the color of wine.

Not their fault, the leavings—mine.

The moon is a wick left damp and lit against my insistent regret and belief in pieces that fit, souls that meet.

I read my daughter fairy tales, watch her fat baby fingers grow slim and pale as fish, rushing me through the pages to the day too soon I buy her first pair of stockings.

Her legs are long, finely shaped, calves strong, and her face is silvery quick, shy as a new moon.

She

The woman Marlene was born to smelled like pepper brown gravy and Tareyton cigarettes and bleach and the olive rich moistness of age. This mother of Marlene never slept because laundry had to be done sometime, and couldn't be done while she ironed sheets and swept floors for someone else to earn that $114.00 a week. The one pleasure she took, silently secretly as if someone might steal it, might stop it, was the newspaper, its ink blackening her fingers already twisted at forty, that newspaper could only be read during time marked by others for sleep. Marlene, belly tight with the urge to pee, knew when she got out of her bed, when she slid out into the coldness rising from the wood floors, that she would see the woman she was born to touch every page of that paper like a hymnal. Marlene hid in the hall, watching this mother ignore the silence growing legs at the door below, watching this woman tighten cheeks bleached and blowsy as rags and pretend against what she knew, where he was, where he always was. Marlene, bladder relieved, looked away, walked away, deliberately not seeing the older woman's lips move as she read, her teeth click clicking like Rosary beads.

The mother never comes to her dreams, so Marlene imagines, reconstructs that narrow kitchen lit only with martyr's light, her mother's suffering stretched, arching and filling, expanding, taking the shape of the demon who tempted Christ on the side of the mountain in her child's Bible, the pain swirling in grays and blacks around her mother's head, toothed and clawed and ravenous. Always at the same point in Marlene's imagining, the woman she was born to falls to her knees, the newspaper forgotten, dropped, and the mother, like Sisyphus, dries that moonstone glaze in circles with a square of frayed red flannel, her hands painting prayer in circles in half circles in ovals in sweeps of her ten fanned fingers *holy mary mother of god pray for us sinners now and at the hour of our death, hail mary full of grace the lord is with thee blessed be thy name and blessed is the fruit of thy womb jesus*

In the daylight now, Marlene finds random tiny red strings sometimes in her bath, and plucks them like unexpected capillaries from smooth white Italian tile.

Neanderthal

The boy she loved in high school, or thought she loved, because he was so insistent, because he pursued her so. Junior year, he followed her to Nags Head even after she had dumped him, risking arrest by walking into her biology class two years after he'd quit to work repairing cars in the daytime, selling meth at night. His mouth powdery, ancient, conquered hers as everyone in Mr. Bullock's class looked on. His insistence confirmed her belief that Neanderthals had not, in fact, vanished, but bred, bowed bone to long femur, coarse into fine, into any number of their taller sisters, homo sapienettes, who laid back accepting his devolved beauty, but only where they wouldn't be seen. After, she moved again to the fires of her own kind, sending him back to scrape hides, believing her birthright came from finer bones, shapelier skull. He must have watched her, seen her satiated. Secretly animalized. That boy, Randy, black eyes beneath ridged brow, led her to the beach below the motel, sand sliding a world away beneath them, his demanding hands showing again and again that he wanted her, wanted her like no one else, her pelvis a dense flat rock worthy of pounding, flint sharp hips against his, bent on making a spark against extinction, shaping a species.

What He Said About a Dancer's Body

She knew he wanted sex but she liked the touching, a slow inventory of his man's body, the physicality of him, the range and variation of angles and planes, the squareness of his hands and feet, the pulled broadness of his back and buttocks, the wide knobs of his spine. She palmed his back, cupped her hand over the wings of his shoulder blades, while he told her of a dancer he'd known when he first came to New York, a Dominican girl named AnnaLee with broad hips and strong legs and small breasts and a waist he could span with his hands. Marlene imagined the salt on his skin while he told her AnnaLee smelled like Africa, like sand and heat and ancient wind, but that she'd left him when she got into that dance school she wanted in Manhattan. But you don't even have a dancer's body, he'd told her, dancers look like boys. AnnaLee had laughed and said, Not Dominican dancers and her laughter, Marlene thought, still hung like webs in the corners of his room, and she imagined her up there, with them, above them dancing, the bending back, the spinning feet, the graceful as black birds hands of a beautiful Dominican woman and Marlene imagined drums and she wanted to dance herself, right then. But she knew he wouldn't dance with her, not even naked, and so fingering the knobs of his spine, one touch at a time, walking down his back from his neck, the hook and lock of the bones wide and pleasing to her and she asked him what she smelled like. You, he said, sliding her farther back, as much as he could on the twin mattress he had shoved in the corner of the efficiency he rented in Brooklyn, you smell like dew and rain and cucumbers. And because she liked him, she didn't mind that he'd talked of this woman he loved, at least he did love, so she walked her fingers down the curved bone anchoring his hip, a curve she planned on biting softly, and she licked at the knobs of his spine as he leaned into her hands, and holding him—them—together, curved and eager, she said you smell like *now*.

At Caddo

we knelt, we women, in living prayer to grind acorns, percussion of bone, horn and stone, flour loosening there beneath our touch, smooth as the mush I chewed, then softened with the pad of my tongue, from marsh elder, to finger into the half moon mouth of the black-eyed child we made. For your house by the red river, I boiled squash and pumpkin, fried fat and deer liver, gathered goosefoot and chinquapins, their woody shells stars you cracked with square strong teeth, the nutmeat spilling sweet from your mouth to mine. In the village, the connas kept time, those priests who played pallilos, who whispered first into the ear of the deer you brought, who taught of ships and open skies, the twin gaze of the feathered snake, the shake, rasp and rattle of the ancestor songs, how the desert stars had always been our eyes, how the desert fires were our fires too. We knew—all along—we women, all time given when we still floated in our mothers' blood, our unformed tongues already brave, speaking to the xinesi of the red sand we would make to honor his grave. My mother, her fingers stained and sticky with first fruit, traced my route across the swollen drum of her own belly, while I swam within, marking the map of all women, the telling like persimmon bite, sweetening only as I grew, then came, finally, in ripeness, to you. You gave me purslane, pulled young and wild, and I tore the woody stem open for its sweet bit of milk, keeping safe the tiny seeds, dark and silky as my skin, in a hide bag, guarding them, always for the planting, for the time we would begin again.

Personal Genomics

for Chuck Ross

Would Houdini have cared for pyrosequencing, nanopore technology laying bare the base illusion, genomes sequenced there, as scraped and raw as epithelial from a liquid tongue, a life undone, completely? Would he have offered up his sperm or spit to get to that final answer, to learn how Sturtevant's magic worked, that twist and tangled angling of the plan, this making of man, snipped his own hair, piece by readable piece? *As, Ts, Cs and Gs*—suppose the design and region, propose to give us what Harry sought, the ultimate reveal. But no map can mark the impossible worlds seen through a pale gypsy eye, the story and ancient why for the shovel-shaped tooth or finger curved to palm with lust or fear, the filled-to-burst heart, the come here linger of blood in thinning veins, no sequence the slow burn of violin strings on skin, the begin and begin again, that child to man to star bursting, like Houdini into history, the shredding of science into human, into mystery.

Announcement

On Monday the principal, Sister Imelda, made an announcement over the loudspeaker. Greg Barnes' father had died. She asked us to pray for his soul, reminding us that Hail Marys were always effective and welcome. Keep the family in your prayers, she reminded and everyone looked at Greg's empty seat and nodded, knowing now why he wasn't there, even though they had a big science test, and somebody, one of the girls, targeting the boys, whispered, yeah, like you don't already pray for his sister. The other girls giggled. Maureen Barnes, Greg's sister, older by two years, was that one girl every thirteen-year-old boy prays for, gone bad early, lacy cup bras with real breasts that everyone knew she let be touched, peeking out of her Dairy Queen uniform when she leaned from the drive-through, handing out frosties and foot-longs. Kenny Small hissed back, well, keep praying yourself. Your own tits'll come in one day. Our teacher, Sister Mary John, clapped her hands and we turned to the board, untangling the table of genus, phylum, species by licking the nubs of our number two pencils and staring out the window. When Greg came back on Wednesday, we followed him around like he was a new kid, someone we never seen before or talked to. That lasted until recess, when Greg simply walked away, across St. Peter's back parking lot, past the monkey bars paid for by bake sales, and toward the highway, where his dad had driven truck for thirty years, passing the school and the Dairy Queen more times in a single lived day than we could even imagine Sister Imelda turning the switch in the main office, the loudspeaker crackling to life.

We Stood With You

Proselyte: Origin: Middle English proselite, from Greek prosēlutos, stranger, proselyte: pros-, pros-+, ēluth-aorist tense stem of erkhesthai, to go, soujourner in a strange land

We stood with you, in that valley of dry bones, placing damp stones between your skeletal teeth, that you might breathe again, skin shimmering back into place like growing new limbs, nightsky cry of dust to rattle and quake, awaken to the truth that we all must: we are all proselytes. Let Gog and Magog battle among themselves, gnaw their own throats, eat their own rancid fruit. Let them burn, as they will. The heavens churn, wheel into wheel, bone to muscle, muscle to flesh, as you feel the call of fresh blood, iron thickening in your mouth, loins quickening for this new birth. You swallow the pebble we placed on your tongue and it cleaves like a star in your chest. You know—it is yours to clean up the mess they leave.

Bear Watches From the Woods

as she carries food, water, grief settled like hot stones in the basin of her belly. From the mist-heavy trees, he sees the missing-him grow into a solid thing between her shoulder blades, new bones there on the shaded side of her heart, arcing up to pierce skin, velvet thin nubs at first, then the feathered fingers of some ancient nameless bird. She sings to herself, some song without words, out of time, and there in the curve of her spine, that line he learned with his tongue, his teeth, drawing her into him in the early between time, first blush of day, she sings and he watches as they grow—her wings, delicate and gray. He knew even before—that they'd grow, the wings she'd always wanted, or thought she wanted, night wings, brushing time and moon aside, grow from depths where he left her. Bereft, she doesn't even know she owns them yet, eyes too wide and wet to see anything save his face in every pale wind. He breathes in, exhales, slowly, his breath trembling the distance between them, and watches as the song stops, caught on hooks in her throat. She looks toward him. He wants her to know the shape of the gift, that time is a funny thing, not so long after all. He wants her to lift on those wings, not to hesitate nor hide, to know that this love abides. He wants her to sing, and she does, all vibration and hue, her song a cool blue call into the deep green where he waits.

If We Could Know Our Bones

But if you do not know yourselves, then you live in poverty. —Gospel of Thomas

If we could know our bones the way we know our skin, perhaps we'd not dig graves, but build rooms, havens, shrines, for even our enemies, their bodies rescued from the ditch and battlefield, no longer pitched into holes, safe and out of sight, but standing, eloquent and equal in their lines: tines of rib, cradle of skull, clavicle like a little key, memories of movement in femur and fluted tibia, their jaws, hinged and singing, angel light pouring through the basin of each pelvis. Free of water, fat and muscle, perhaps they'd claim us, tell us of sharing even what can't be known, *Os innominatum*—those nameless bones.

Synesthesia

The unity of the senses doctrine states that there exists common dimensions upon which all senses exist. —American Synesthesia Association

1

My perceptual purdah, permeable curtain that makes your voice on the phone a shimmering chocolate color, remembered from that summer so long ago; you were chocolate even then. Sound is color, light is sound, has always been, my mother's voice a silvery-gray, my father's call deep green, the brother I loved who passed away too soon, calling and chasing there on the dirt path behind me, his laugh a sudden boom, fall and scatter of pennies, bright copper sparks on the air. I dug today, with my hands, for coins in the dirt, knowing I'd not find any.

2

This multi-layering of consciousness tears down bearing walls, turns me over in crowded train stations, ignites my brain in airports, voices fall like fireworks, report like shotgun cracks, trembling trails of reds that burn, my eyes, my skin, I taste what I know is the color of my heart, frantic blooded animal panicked within the cage of my ribs. I tell myself breathe, breathe, sing, sing now. I've been drowning, swimming, in tie-dyed air since I first learned how to see.

3

The first time I recall, at three, sitting between my grandpa's knees at the piano. He struck a key, and I saw blue, another, green. He played chords, amber, teal and crimson. Chopsticks was a candy-cane, Clair de Lune a score of ribbons.

4

I photograph reflections on the surface of water, listen to the light and lap, until I hear a color, feel texture against my skin or taste timing like ice cream, liquid motion, a dream gone real there in the frame, what this *condition* as they name it, positions me to see and hear, all at once, like a fish trapped in ice, time in topographical maps, the clear blue ringing of stones, guitar strings yellow and hot, the lavender sound of a flute as it sings, and you, voice ancient and smoky as chocolate.

Dimes

Saturday night is the loneliest night of the week. Frank Sinatra said so. And if Frank said it, my father believed it. His angled jaw shaved close with the straight razor we weren't allowed to touch, then he became again the smooth Slow Joe Murphy folks around Brooklyn knew before Pop was Pop. His broad red face softened when he crooned *My Way* to my brother Bobby in the crib set up in the front of the living room window to catch the breeze. Down the fire escape, the smacking sound of Norman Watts beating his wife Chauncey carried easy on the curling ascending waves of concrete heat. Mom stopped for a minute over the sizzle of Polish sausage in her blackened skillet, splitting their reddened skins and spitting grease up on to her fingers. Little blisters rose shiny as dimes on the back of her hands when Chauncey's voice carried too clear through the window. Norman, no! The paint on the fire escape was black and flaked and when Bobby got older, we peeled off little pieces to get to the gray primer underneath. We pretended it was a pirate ship. Or a get-away car. By then, Chauncey had died, her head bent, misshapen, caught in the rungs of the ladder outside their second floor window and Norman Watts carted away by black-shoed Irish cops my Pop knew from sharing a pint at The Shadow Box. Bobby asked me last week when he brought his daughter over for me to watch if I remembered eating supper on the end of Mom and Pop's bed in the apartment in Flatbush. Remember Mom hugging Pop in the flicker of the streetlight, calling him Slow Joe when they danced on the fire escape, he asked. His daughter, hair wispy and blonde as Bobby's had been, ran to find my boys, shouting Let's play pretend, let's play pretend. Bobby left, crooning softly to himself, and the children started their game, their eyes round, and shiny as dimes.

This Bread, Those Beans

for Bear

Resistance is the thief—surrender is the gift giver.   —*Guru Singh*

This bread, those beans, the meat you slice and feed to me from the shining point of your knife, lean and charred, it slips between my lips to my tongue, salted as generations of hard men sweating up through you. I cannot lift my fingers; they linger, curled to cups in my lap. I cannot raise my eyes higher than the square ride of your man's hips, buttocks fitted for horse, for hides, for snow-dead winters of bearing what men know: that work fills the rough ache of empty hands, that fear resides in blood and bone, and redemption hides in the small of a lover's back, that the lack of that one woman's touch will break the strongest man, stone to ash, oak to tinder. Your thumb traces the points of my teeth. The gifts you bring—blanket, beef—on the table between us, this, we both know, is surrender, its form wide and old as sky. I take your knife from your fist, and press its curved cold blade against my thigh, until it warms.

The Food She Makes Him

she still cuts in tiny bites, Ahi tuna almond soaked, sesame slick and shiny, nori wrap blooming from the pads of her fingers, until each seam gleams from her mother's touch. She pinces sticky rice, each grain twice-rinsed, to free the starch, to feed this son, strengthen the march of those infant legs she recalls, the thump and pull as he swam up from the hollow sway beneath her ribs. Her hand cupped on her belly, back then she imagined him a sharp-tailed shrimp, frothy pink curl of flesh, anemone in a sweetened sea. He belongs to me, she had whispered, hollowing melon with the bowl of her spoon. Giving she knows. It means to live. So even now, dumplings grow fat and rich in broth, aji, sweet pickles, salted cod, daikon, miso ball for soup. He will always want miso, when he comes. She'll boil water later, fry enoki, eggplant, as good as that wife might wish she could make, that wife who keeps him, so far away, for years now, in a city she's never seen, where she knows, just knows, the Ahi is never fresh, the nori dying from lack of salt and water.

On Not Being Carried

Joanna rises from a green and white nylon lawn chair. The chair's front legs bend, so that when she stands, it groans beneath her weight, then spills on to summer grass bleached the color of bone. Softly she talks about her old life as the simple facts. Shifting across the yard to where clumps of sweet basil bunch in the shade, beneath the one live oak the yard boasts, she bends to test the leaves, recalls growing up back in Indian Woods. Times when her African grandfather faked his own death, his breath slowed in his chest. Slow, slower. Stopped. She'd press her cheek pressed against the frame of his ribs, whistle across his striped cotton pajamas stained redbone with drips of chew. Back then, she whistled breath beneath the buttons, listening for what she wasn't sure. A clear heartbeat. Returning seep of air from his lips.

Lawd, lawd, Joanna, come here!

Mama, he's sleep.

No, no, no.

Her mama called to the girl she was then, yawning, sitting half on the toilet, half off, child's body pressed against the wall. Mama rushed the hall, wheezing, scared, red.

Joanna, come here! Make him be undead again.

Before that her fast-talking cousin braided her hair in a basement shop in Windsor. Scalp oiled and pulled, she dream-walked worlds away from there, away from that grandfather's place, from the burnt black smell of straightener, grease, and dust gathering in the shop corners. Now beneath the oak, she pulls at the curled ends of her cropped hair, pinches the basil back to keep it coming, paints them all—mama, sister, grandfather, self—living together in a shotgun shack on that plot of slaved soil her great-grandmama worked.

"Did ya know," she asks, "cotton burrs, how when they're cold, you can't feel the blisters growin until they burst?" They'd bury the blood-speckled bolls in the bottom of the burlap bag, hidden beneath the weight of pure white. Her great-grandmama bled like that, she says, but never pretended dying. Her owner wouldn't have stood for it.

Four generations free, she pinches tufts of sweet large-leafed basil, spiny sage, and talks sometimes of the Cherokee daddy she never knew but figures the cinnamon tone of her skin—reckon it comes from him. Staring past the sage, beyond the herb yard to the cracked blacktop gone clay soft in the summer sun, she mentions that other California grandmother who never claimed anyone, much less her. "We oughta get inside now," she says. "Can't you smell the rain that's coming?"

In the dim house, she burns pulled sage in a black painted pot on the table for the smoke, speaks about its healing, how new cilia will grow in the lungs if you sit and breathe it. And the Cherokee grandmother?

"No never mind that now." She walks the floor for matches, to relight the green sage, knows there are larger things to find, but needs the circle of smoke hanging like lace lining the air. She opens drawers and mutters about matches rattling around here somewhere.

Another time, an evening that makes her smile to remember, on a porch summers ago when the grass was damp and scattered with the pinched armor of vanished crickets and cicadas clicked against the wood spindles, her great-grandmother's magnolia wept slick perfume across the air. And Granddaddy was there, and breathing. Mama and her sister Kat sang *Rugged Cross* while somehow, from her corner of the porch—she didn't know how—but she was leaving.

That was her first dream-flight, across the yard, above the magnolia, rolling over and over into a twilight where jackrabbits appeared, even little ones, feeding on a broken ledge of sky edged with Cherokee beading. Digging matches finally from the heart of a drawer, beneath Kat's medicine refills and her mama's disability forms, she retrieves the light she needs and tells you, "We buried Granddaddy for real that year."

She strikes the small flint, doesn't give up until it catches, says she wants to finish learning the Cherokee words for *Rugged Cross*. The empty book of matches flaps open, wings on the padded ends of her fingers, while outside the window, it just does begin to rain.

"Tsalagi means the people," she says, "what the Cherokee call themselves. I found me a book with the Cherokee alphabet and when I learn some more—"
From the back of the house, a voice calls out. *Joanna! Come here—I need you.*

She slips the smoldering wand back into the little black pot, pads away down the dusky hall.

She looks back once, and asks, "You know how it is, right? To need?"

Sometimes the words she doesn't know burn in her head at night, when she's lying alone in a bed floating a few inches about the floor, and you know without being told that the whole room smells of sage.

Marooned

The habit is simple. I'm a junkie for marooned men. As friends, as lovers, as close as the nearest juke joint, Walmart, banks, bowling alleys. Sometimes it takes nothing more than a good average to draw me in. They never went to prison first, waited until they had me solid, stoned on the I'm-gonna-be-the-one-only-I-can-save-him-kind of love that grows from the seeds of a father's distance, in the soil of a mother's anger. Dreams and Marlboros tucked into a jute green bag, I danced lawns and lawn boys, swept the bottoms of pools for them as they praised my ass, bent doing their work, mechanic, academic, tragic as James Dean, clean as a whistle is what they picked me. But then again, I picked them. You can't swim away when you're an intentional castaway, a buoy with a sharpie smile, a shifting tropical isle of your own making, undulating shorelines, exactly the right curves, ones that everything slides off of and away from, with no corners on which anything permanent can ever really find a place to catch. And hold.

He

The man Marlene was born to cocked his 38 at hamburgers frying in Crisco and hurled shoes at shadows outside the torn screen door, then slid sock-footed on the white glaze that slicked the Pine Sol mopped linoleum and old turquoise Frigidaire, wetting the lilac-papered hallway with fingerprints lit by a single stubborn ceiling bulb that Marlene never once remembered anyone changing. This man she was born to, though, swore he had style, wore diamond pinky rings on his soft Irish hands, lit cigarettes as if the flame grew from his smooth thumb, and tossed women's hats out push-button El Dorado windows, just for sport. He tipped big cabbage-rolls of cash, tilting toe to toe like Sinatra and smiling down at his own face in his polished wing tips, hanging with Billy Pip at The Shadow Box bar, buying rounds for the regulars who called him Mikey the Dancer.

When he comes to Marlene's dreams, he is not under the influence running naked up the stairs, hard-on wagging in anger at his hatless Polish wife who piously scrubbed past midnight, waiting for the sound of his boots falling thud thud to the floor. When he comes to her dreams, he is bleary-eyed and veiny, teeth-stained rubber from nicotine and liver. His fingers sticky with Jameson's and wads of gambling tender reeking of cheap cigars and Aqua Velva, he weeps to Danny Boy. Crying, he hands her Moon Pies. And she is no longer the baby grinding her tiny pearl teeth to sand.

Bread

Mama makes bread when Daddy makes trouble. I sit in the corner and watch when the sheriff brings Daddy home from old Joe's poker house. He's drunk again and Mama thanks the sheriff kindly before closing the door on the night outside. Mama says "Go to bed, Luci" and Daddy says "Come here, baby" but most times, I go to bed 'cause I know that's what's best by the look in Mama's brown eyes. Daddy says "Come here, baby" over and over again until I am at the top of the stairs and Mama's voice is a hiss far away as the spit of the stove. I get in bed with my yellow quilt and picture all the bread we'll have for breakfast. They're yelling by then and I can tell when Daddy's losing 'cause he changes "Come here, baby" to "Aw, Honey." I know Mama's pulling dough in her hands, flour scattered white, powdering the breadboard. I try to stay awake but the smell of fresh bread wafts around me warm and slow and when my eyes close, I dream of the seeds in blackberry jam getting stuck in my teeth and my fingers slipping on the slick buttery crust of braided bread. In the morning, I never ask where Daddy is. I don't want to know if Mama let him sleep here or made him go down the road to Uncle Ray's. I just slide my chair in close to the table, remember not to spread crumbs around, and use my napkin to wipe jam from the corners of my mouth. The bread is French this time, long even loaves lined on the counter and Mama lets me climb in a chair beside her while she slices it in thick spongy pieces. "Good girl" is what she says 'cause I'm careful to stand in the middle of the chair. Mama's hair is soft and dark when it spills against my arm. She kneads and kneads some more. The air is warm around us with the smell of yeast bubbling, sun rising.

In the Jungle You Discover

beneath your skin, bird bone, brittle as light, a riddle of otters, cacophony of owl and hoatzin; big cats with eyes like stone, eyes like rubies, roar the rainstorm in your belly awake. Take it, they say. Raucous flutter of wings under water, you are both fish and fowl, diving into the dark swirl of the Urubamba where frog princes keep singing til you come. So come. Dip, dive again. Howl. Hunt. Fingers in mouth, in cunt, trailing the skin-thin surface of that one mate, who rises like steam off the aguas calientes;   Tanager, Macaw, Trainbearer, Trogon—no, he is Cock of the Rock, famed Peruvian lover who favors the morning, jumping, preening, beak snapping until you are won over; this is his gift to you, freedom to be all: leggy as the tiger-heron, free and fierce, slippery and open and ancient as fish we can no longer name.

When My Dead Father Comes to Visit

When my dead father comes to visit, he wears a white hat, jaunty I guess you'd call the way it's tilted on his head. He always shows up with wicker furniture on the back of a truck. Then my Brooklyn dad, who never drove a truck, pops the tailgate like a pro, saying *Good to see ya, I missed you, ya know.* The furniture is a gift, he says, for my new house, a house I bought eight years after he passed. I help him unload a large cabana chair, its back arched like *wings* he says, *like yours.* I touch my collarbone, bend my arm back, fingers to scapula, just checking, because if my dead father can visit, I think maybe I could have grown wings and not known it. *Gotcha,* he says, laughing that sharp as glass laugh that carried him through five heart attacks, two strokes, and open heart surgery twice, carried him to that last night when he touched my mother's cheek, called her *Rock,* sighed once deeply, and went to sleep forever.

Gotcha, he says again, and now two wicker tables appear. He lifts the large chair as if it's cotton, butter, air, and motions impatiently for me to take the tables, so I do, and follow, wondering if I'm dreaming or if in Virginia, the rules are different than in North Carolina where I grew up, so different that it's not unusual to follow your dead father into a house he's never seen. He's younger than I've ever known him, in his twenties, and suited up, a skinny skinny black tie over a glaring white shirt. I've seen him younger like this in pictures, shots of him as an altar boy in Brooklyn, his older brother, my uncle the priest beaming behind him, then in a ducktail pose from St. Francis' Prep, the place that led him to seminary, the holy study he left to marry my mom. But I've never seen him so—I don't know—*smooth.*

Inside, he mutters as he sets the wicker chair down on my hardwood floors, curses in Gaelic as if it's heavy, although the chair floats to the floor. He points, showing me where he wants me to put the tables, and then shoves his hands in his pockets, jingling change like I remember he did when he was nervous.

I know you miss the beach, he says, *the water. I thought this stuff might help.* Then he turns to leave, my back door standing open, filled with light, and I say "*Wait, Daddy, I—*"

He stops in the door, and he smiles, a smile so large it folds into in his eyes, but says softly, *How 'bout we don't tell your mother I stopped by, maybe we'll keep it just between us.*

And he goes, across the deck, back to a truck he never owned. At my back door, I just watch, not asking where he is now, or how it is he comes to visit, or why he keeps bringing the same wicker furniture so I won't miss the beach. All I can think as my
dead father drives away is that next time I need to ask him where he got the hat.

The Dove That Calls

there into the dew, in the air folding into morning, knew the secrets of light would not come without warning. She has held time beneath her wings, and those years resonate with the sounds of caves singing, of first feet on a beach, of gods who fluttered just within our reach, if only we'd lifted our eyes. The sound of soil seduces, the sift and silt of sand, ribs of undertow reducing the space we know, and the dove from deep in the stand of pines and cypress, calls to the bones of our memory, *listen, listen, don't go.*

Placing

The apples don't last. She buys them anyway, carries them home from the market in a bag, places them one at a time, gingerly into the gray bowl, their skins blush against the ceramic. She knows they won't last. Only a week in the bowl and they go soft. Their skins will loosen like her body on the days she loves it least.

They're organic, she tells her friend. And it's true. But tonight these apples know more than she does. The book in her lap, pages unseen, the tips of her fingers grow as red as the apples were. Tonight, the apples know what she hasn't learned yet. How to go on, ripening soundlessly on the first night of winter, assuming the shape of the clay bowl that holds them.

Some nights she is so tired it is hard to continue. And though she knows it is only the patch of darkness grafted on her heart, she can't find a place safe or still enough to stand in, the circle of light that held the mice in her favorite children's book eluding her as it eluded Cheerful, the one with the white feet who wanted to live in the country. So she puts the book, still open, aside, pads through the winter silence in her house and prepares for the day to come. There are four posts around my bed, there are four angels 'bout my head, Matthew, Mark, Luke and John, bless the bed I lie on, the church mice sang *The White Paternoster* as they played hide and seek in the vestry. And everybody was happy but Cheerful, who stood in the pool of green cast through the stained glass, imagining meadows. And even then she too wanted to be elsewhere. And even then her father recognized something, buying the book for her after they'd checked it out of the Hatteras Public Library ten times. He pulled the book from inside his coat, from where he'd protected it against the sudden but expected July rain just beyond the door, and handed it to her. Putting words and travel in her hand, though they already lived in the country.

We know the way, the voices sang in the story, guiding Cheerful home. This is the path. And though there was no reason to believe, she did. When she opened the book, she was home. And though she wants to remember, to render it accurately, she cannot find it when she goes to check the library shelf that holds the books of her girlhood, Little House on the Prairie, or In the Big Woods, The Ghost at the Window, Irish Tales for Children, everything there but Cheerful, its small pages dog-eared from a child's sticky hands.

 She had no reason to believe anything. But she did. As she wants to again when she looks for the book, when she bites through the tart skin of one of the apples, and finds the meat firm, white, and sweet, as unspoiled as the world was then, though she cannot remember how unspoiled feels, only the circle of lamplight the dark in her persists in leaving. And she sets out again. She is always setting out, the inside of her head a torrent of petals, familiar as this hard nurture her stuck tongue calls rain. She knows the story ends happily, but even walking the house in the dark again and again, she cannot find where she placed it.

Words Like River, November

Words like *river, November, moon*, they seize you, close their fingers around your throat, like that beloved who leaves, lifetime after lifetime, his giving and going sooner and older than starlight and fancy; words like *tremble* and *memory*, almost caught words, words like *chance*, like the rosary that's all that's left of your mother, deceptive depth of green marble, Connemara cold no matter the heat of your hands; words like *other, listen, jungle*, meet you at the door, all doors, teeth clicking like beads, skinned drums for feet, they dare you to *understand,* to climb the temple steps, words like *stumble, recovery* and *lover*, they greet you at the burning top of the mound with words that sound like *forget, genetics* and *jaguar*. You are. The word *you* a constellation, from *thou* to *ye* to fifteenth century streets cobbling into the verb *to be*. Words like *now* and *time* and *see* and *life*. Words like *sacrifice*, from the Latin, *sacrificium*, from *sacrifico*, from *sacer + facio*, which means *to make sacred*. And you know that word; it's yours, and you'll take it.

Writ During War

It's not for you to know, but for you to weep and wonder. —Neko Case

When the words first appeared on her infant's skin, the mother scrubbed and scrubbed, imagining that she was imagining, imagining someone—something—sliding in when she wasn't looking to scribble the verses, beginning with the name of the Creator on the curve of his cheek. Red and raised, the verses on his legs spoke obedience, peace words curved his belly, the telling of the history of Believers inscribed on his back, glowing then fading, rising with the weekend and the sun. She swaddled him at first, afraid, she wrapped his legs, tucked brushed cotton in over his feet even as prayers for the wicked wrapped his thighs like rose-colored vines, even as the rumors began to simmer, then roil, when she couldn't hide his written skin in the market or on the street. *Liar's ink*, they grumbled, *blasphemy*, they said, blaming the parents for seeking fame, or fortune, the voices growing louder and louder, rumbling so that it drowned even the roar of the war around them. the missiles and guns, the cries of the dead and half-dead in hospitals, all forgotten, as the mystery of the infant grew. *Lo and be healed* called the pilgrims out, from the alleys and villages, from the cities with the white buildings reaching into the sky like fingers, from the hills and sea they came, by the thousands, in cars and on buses wailing and waiting to see the child. They called for him to be brought to them, for his body to be read, for his tears to be collected, in clay cups, in bowls blessed by the priests, so that they might be healed from the raw open skin of phosphorous burns, the bones shattered, fragments of bombs weeping beneath torn skin, the brain tissue shivered to ribbons, demons seeping into the air before their eyes. His mother no longer scrubbed, the prayer words now coming faster on his small body than she could conceal, words rising and replacing themselves as she hung thicker and thicker curtains, darker and darker wool, on all the windows, against the thunder of warheads, the pleading of pilgrims—*surely goodness and mercy shall follow you....* In the dim room, she sat, humming, and held him, his mouth lax in sleep, his lips milky, one tiny bloom of a fist on her chest, holding her heart in place.

Funeral Food

Tuna casserole, I hear, up north, pasta salad. Down here, we bake, something sweet: Red Velvet cake, coconut macaroons singed to gold, Key Lime pie. Potholders fold around the oven-hot edges of macaroni and cheese, Sunday style, Ritz crackers crushed in butter strewn across the top, all sewn together with strings of cheddar that ride the air between your fork and your mouth. Deviled eggs sparked with paprika, biscuits stuffed with ham, all pyramid the table as mourners move from room to room, their voices dark as the coffee brewing, the tea waiting, sweet and thick, in the fridge. An aunt, a grandmother, a neighbor who doesn't know what else to say, sets a platter of chicken on the table. "I'm not the fryer in the family," she starts out. "Now Sarah, she could sure fry chicken. What you want to do is salt and pepper it right. Soak it in milk good, before you flour it. Then you want to cook it in hot grease. You can use Crisco or you can use the liquid, it doesn't matter. We always used Crisco. But anyway, you want to cook it in enough hot grease. Sarah did that." She wipes her hands on her skirt, elbows in tight to her pocketbook, then murmurs away, leaving behind her condolences, legs, breasts, thighs, and wings. The screen door bangs behind her like a shotgun crack, and every soul in the room wants to follow her, kick the dust in the yard, jump the car alive, and run, gun it, until the engine squeals and the tires burn. But we wait, surrounded by food, for the passing to pass, the house humming around us, we listen for the released breath after the viewing, the scritch of that handful of dirt done tossed, then quietly slapping palms, shaking that dust loose, we go home to our own families, touch them when they're not looking, start up our own dinners. We make potato salad, milky with mayonnaise, a bite of mustard, and enough onion to make your eyes burn, to make you cry.

Upon Waking I Remembered

that place we walked, those suns, that sky, littered with shreds of story, where we learned to fly, silent pairing of wings the only thing that mattered, I met you at the peak, lavender glory shining to us, through us, especially in that first glancing touch, scattered soulspeak the song you sang, forever filling me. There we learned to see—when raven gave us the stone, picked from the bones of our jaws, the sand in our cheeks, streaks of granite and sky, we took it, thrumming of veins in our eyes, your fingers lacing all time into mine. You turned and said, Here, come always here—to me. I lifted my face to you, heart lit heat from the south, parting my lips, and said, Here, take the stone from my mouth.

Catfish

When I was ten and she was twenty, and the only village we knew was a handful of water-stained single-wides cluttering tobacco sand, my sister taught me how to skin a catfish. She scoffed at the size of the bullhead I'd caught, but took the large cat from my hold, *I'll show you, give it to me*. With two strokes of a ballpean hammer, she shot a ten-penny nail clean and fine through the v-shaped skull, pinning it to a pine, tail beating against the scratchy bark. *They're scavengers, Annie, you know that. Trash-eaters, bottom feeders.* Hammer exchanged for a curved skinning knife, she scored then slashed the cat's thick hide, peeled it back still damp, to reveal white muscly meat just below brain matter that fried purple to gray in the summer heat. *Now you.* Her well-kept nails tapped their impatience, as I rolled off the hide, leaving the cat white and bald, me frightened as she said, *Watch the sting. What?* I asked too late, one large tentacle burning a half-moon on to the back of my hand, fire hooking to bone. It seems strange, that same sister, now queen of a small suburban village, gated, convenes every Monday night, when she and her sorority sisters drool over the college boy waiter at Chili's, bemoan their white-collar husbands and discuss how to clean marble properly. Foyers are, after all, the first thing one sees. Sipping kahlua, she watches the young waiter's uniformed thighs stroke across the dining room toward them, raises one hand, and promises them all the number for her marble crew. *The best, you'll see.* The waiter fishtails toward her, sloe-eyed, low-slung and free—she lifts her empty glass and smiles. *Thank you, young man.* That summer thirty years ago, she walked away, laughing, called me a baby as the fish flailed. Then the nail loose, the cat fell, one last attempt at escape, writhing for water, but drowning in sand.

Encounter With Realism as a Child

The toad hadn't moved, hadn't twitched, hadn't wiggled, not even once, not when she stubbed it with the toe of her new white sneaker, not even when she poked it with a stick. The flashlight in her hand held it there, its stubby hind legs splayed and frozen, its yellow eyes staring and round, a statue she thought, between the rock and the water oak, where she'd trapped it with the light just as twilight purpled them both. She dropped the stick, pulled the jackknife from her pocket, and considered her options. The pictures in her science book, the glossy transparencies that layered over each other, she lifted again and again, starting with the toad's bumpy skin, and turning pages through the multicolored digestive and respiratory systems, passing the reproductive organs, until she came to the toad's core, its tiny shovel-shaped skull and bent legs more resembling a bat than an amphibian, a primitive mystery of mechanism, motion. Her fingers sweated around the knife as she opened it, blade silvered, and she stared down at the toad's glistening eyes, skin muddy-green and dry as bark, and especially the curve of its neck, the image she had studied in the book, knowing that that soft stretch of skin would be the starting point, the place her knife would carve the X allowing her to find her way in, to see in three ancient dimensions. She knelt, the ticked point of her blade closing in, the hypnotic beam of light pinning the toad in place, paralyzing it completely, for exploration, she thought, to turn the pages for real this time.

Six Rules for Devils

Emerge where the sand has little salt, in times when gods are forgiven, and bind those you find sweetly, for they twist themselves so much more than we can do, tearing their own skin away from the rashness of knowing. Give them warning, even if they won't listen, their minds too swollen with the wanting of grace. Avoid Gadarenes. You'll not do well there. But do not let them sleep; teach them the beauty of burning, that passion is the taste of their own plum souls.

What Took Root

when that lightning hit? Fingers of light and heat bent around her spine, lifting her skyward, spinning her, thinning her skin into a vortex of time and choice. Choose, he said, choose you, his voice a place she'd been before, in her head, on the heated streets of Cairo, on a hill as she opened beneath him behind that farm in Montana. Remember, he whispered, his breath tender in that bar in Tuscaloosa where he'd slid lime into her mouth, then licked tequila from her collarbone, where they'd danced alone in an alley while a horn somewhere crooned, vibrating through brick and stone, tendrils of song blue and reaching, upward, into night sky and history, long and sweet that mystery—home, she flowered, rose toward him, toward what they knew, had always known, to be theirs, to be true.

Women Now and the Trick of Avoiding Touch

Wandering through Sunday afternoon crowds by the river, obliged to come to some sticky end, she locks her knees, draws breath up beneath her ribs, fearing the sudden warmth under the sheets, skin against skin, afraid for a moment she will repulse him. Power could not reside all in one room, whatever their illusions. A maintenance agreement, they call it, she calls it, whenever he tries to add something, only this giving in for a moment, this letting go, his weight, his chest, his thrust pinning her into place, returning her soul to her body, forcing it back to where she can hold it, control it. His shirt takes the shape of the chair it hangs on, the seat in the same shadows that cleft his collarbone, his knee, the largeness of him above her and she closes her eyes, wordlessly receiving, only what she needs, not more, no matter how he offers, his lips on her upper arm, whispering for some level of trust she hasn't unpacked in years. She's confident this will work. She will make it work, maintaining the trick of avoiding touch. After all, what really can replace the heat of your hands at the crucial moment? Roles crumble, she slides on her jeans and opens the door, the room darker and darker behind her.

This Picture of Himself

for Liam Rector

He grows each time I look at the picture, ten, twenty, hundreds of times bigger than he was even in life, each pixel enlarged and voluminous, like the cells in his body swollen with time and want, like atoms luminously engorged on the air, round and mysterious as marbles, growing until I think I can walk right through him, as he grows beyond quantification, evolves into myth. The questions I want to ask him seem puerile, whiny, so I imagine a parallel existence, Everett's many-worlds proven, where he never smoked that last one, never danced the Mashed Potato, never wrote the long long notes on how it should wind into dramatic conclusion. I stare through the photo into infinite relative states of *himness,* existing in a superposition of two or more possible states of being, of different locations and orientations of spin, the poems still coming, the challenges unrelenting, the shoes worn from his sheer velocity. Or else, he is all electricity, blue-hot and wanton, wild on the wires, scalding the east coast, chain-lightning in his constant travels from Virginia to Vermont, settling only in New York, like a halo, like slight shock from the carpet, a kiss to the feet, a trill up the arm of the woman he loved.

Bad Moon

for Catherine Parnell

When you speak of paradise, I think of Carolina heat lacing the air, beached Southern mamas and babies unloading bologna and Cheerwine and pimiento cheese from the cooler in the trunk of a hubcapped Pontiac. In those moments of memory, I taste salted sand on the tongue, sullen and sudden as baptism and hide my ideas of perfect beneath the broad curled leaf of tobacco, under a sky wide and burnt white by a sun hanging lower than hell on the globe. Home is a kind of forgetting, a way to hope, like walking in a thunderstorm and praying to get struck. You show me Canada, pictures of granite beaches, where sand has to be hauled in, where the sky curves sharply north and the green is history dense. Over the years, the photos of Andy, your cousin whose face I already know somehow, carries wisdom like a yoke on his shoulders, in the loose don't-give-a-fuck hold of his smoke and I like best the ease I see in you there, when your chin tips up instead of ducking, and you sprawl your lean beauty on that broad stage of stone, rather than tucking away in more acceptable patterns. This is what matters. You shiver in the sweet smiling recall of cold water, and even wear the bite of the boat, that tiny fracture of legbone, like a line on the map that will take us anywhere, everywhere—*into the open*. Separate hemispheres, ya know? Those Canadian seas swim in you and over you, and I understand then that it is the sea we share. We have, my friend, traveled under some bad moon, as women do, at times, in the wake of all those who inhabit us, serving to reflect. Reflect. Everyone wants to go to paradise, but I don't believe it, friends and relatives disappearing into hills and haunts and hunts and hurt, and even those who come back can't be sure that what they find will last. When someone says paradise, I shudder at thunderheads over the ocean, its gray steely as the barrels my brothers burned trash in, smoke silky and rotten and old, and I think of the map of the Canadian coast pinned to your door, and the cold, the Atlantic sea currents we hold in common, so deep it swallows that bad moon whole.

That Mother in Gaza

has only a few red lentils, her clay pot filled mostly with water. No bread for the soup, but she prays, words reaching back to Mureybit, to Jericho, where generations knew what it meant to be grateful for food at all. She imagines the mothers then, making *conchis*, lentils cooked with the pods, nothing wasted. As she must do now, even as explosions tremble throughout the city, the tear of machine gun fire and the white-smoke after-math of phosphorus bombs. She measures carefully, minutes and resources. Flour is scarce; she has a spoon or two of oil. Sugar is gone. As the children sleep, she recalls family suppers in safer times, crushing tomatoes and garlic and peppers for *dagga*, olives from her father's farm, baking spicy shrimp in the clay pot her mother gave her. But for now, she soaks the lentils for tomorrow, to speed their cooking, to save the smallest hiss of gas, afraid that, soon, when the borders are sealed, there will be no gas either. The children toss and whimper, pressed close to her, their mouths open flowers she must continue to feed. Their small bodies, bones fragile and fluttery as birds just beneath the skin, curve instinctively, even in sleep, against the sudden explosion of bombs, the rain of gunfire and gaping yaw of missiles. Today, her husband came back from looking for bread, only to tell her that her childhood village, some fifteen houses, groves of citrus and olive, a place where the families laughed while they shared one well, worked together to tend the chickens, and a few head of cattle, all—all—were gone. A single donkey survived, but barely. He did not bring it back. They can't feed it. She swirls her fingers in the cool water, lentils rolling like red tears from her hands, and prays for an hour of electric tomorrow, if only to pump water. The taps, too, are dry. She straightens against the weight of weariness bowing her back, and draws breath a thousand years old. When the children wake, she will have them all make a *dua*. They will ask God for help and mercy, even though she doesn't know what the bombing, what any of this, even means anymore.

After the Owl at Chauvet, Taino

Chauvet, Taino, in your sweet dark places, our shadows brushed notes into stone, song stories for your own, arelto dance we called to you when hands were wings, when tongues were young, when you knew us, knew our owl eyes were your punctuating door, the colon before the list of truest things.

When the Dark Comes

The only reason for time is so that everything doesn't happen at once. —Einstein

When the dark comes, in the dreaming, there is always a flock of birds, sometimes swans, necks stretched like question marks, smooth lines, in pairs, punctuating the murky surface of some unknown pool of water; sometimes there are starlings, flock lifting all at once, rustle of tattered black silk, as sudden as the milky autumnal failing of the light, rising and falling and swooping into the face of a dim sky, and she wants to fly with them, be gone to where there is warmth, and water. Sometimes it is people that flock together, hunched against the howl of weather, by concrete lakes going dry, bowls of bread in their hands for the birds, but no one speaks, or cries, all of them silent, even her, and she checks her pockets, for keys, for reasons, for butterscotch candy, yellow as spring, for anything handy that might call the birds back, but it is a long night of empty pockets, of spaces with no fill, of sky that turns itself away, even still her own fingers turn to featherless wings, and she knows the crude truth, the sting of her own limited primitive mind; and yet, still she reaches, desperate hoot and call, flapping and clawing at whatever shredded light she can find.

To Water, From Water

Every man carries within himself the history of the world. —Montaigne

Not what you think, that call of sea to skin, pull of tide between your thighs, eddy and sluice of blood in veins, breasts rising with the tug of moon—not myth, but memory. *Hear me.* Remains of history in my bath, in my kitchen, guiding the point of my knife as I free the oyster from its shell. They rise, gods of fin and foam, broad and sky-eyed, Oannes, dark gulf waters shadow the bell of her singing hips, swirl his chest wide as solace. *You know.* They speak, seeking tongue to bone, you know the geometry of the temple wall, leaven for three hundred breads, how to call the mollusk from the stone. You know to salt the meat and soak the fruit in honey. You know which oil will bring the slow burn, to turn and taste the lowland soil for ash prior to planting. You know the sin in waste, and to follow the hunter's lines to what is holy. I return to water, hold the oyster firmly in one hand, and break the seal, slip the silvery blade into the hinge, pry and twist, reveal the meat. I know the muscle clings, tight until I cut it; undone, the oyster floats, the brine is sweetly sharp, stings like knowing on my tongue.

Talking in Tongues

For anyone who speaks in a tongue does not speak to men but to God. —Paul, First letter to the Corinthians, Verse 14:2

She did not know the Greek *glossa* for *tongue* and *lalia* for *talk*, just the Carolina preachers who said God made the night this dark so she'd know her sin, that sin held back only by the words given her, witness to believer, believer to God, ecstatic, to dance beseeching, not just a single utterance of strange words but a recurrence of such utterances in a series, not to be translated, nor learned. The men who came to her from the farm and the factory heard only the call of her sex, paid no mind to the words as they trekked from the shot-house up the plank roads to the single lamp she kept burning through an oilpaper window, thin light threading the way through the cypress to the swamp. Men of dirt and lumber, deprived of miracles, paid no mind to her babble and moan, mouthed her breasts, chewed at the curved cup of her belly, while she grappled with the secrets of the telling. Like the Camisards or Waldensians, she took Paul at his word, clawing her own flesh and theirs into Acts of fire, tongues of light, seeking redemption, she speaking leagues, while ruddy-faced men plowed away the weight of hard hurt lives, the language of God himself rising between her thighs.

It

The child Marlene didn't have, chose not to have, appears in her dreams, pink, always pink, curled like a shrimp, tiny as a shrimp, frothy and tailed as a shrimp; other times,
she is a tiny blind fish, silver and skin thin as light, white as light, her salmon colored mouth open and suckling and searching. Always in water, that baby, just beneath the surface, that daughter, where light bends her tiny baby face, folds her features in halves, then in quarters. Sometimes, Marlene kneels and tries again and again to catch her, to lift her from the water to the light, her hands dipping in again and again, the soft skin inside her wrists frigid from the fast moving stream or bath or tumble of water just before the rocks, the rocks that Marlene keeps watching, knowing their edges, knowing their dangers, and those rocks that seem to grow closer and closer the more often she slides her hands into the depths where the folding keeps happening, keeps distorting the face she should have known, and Marlene tastes salt and iron, her tongue brining in her own mouth, until the smooth as glass stones shatter, spinning around them like stars, burning around Marlene like stars, blinding her until she looks down and sees the water is gone, has ebbed away, her fingers clawing into dry sand.

The Marine at the Bowling Alley

didn't want to talk about Iraq, no matter how many hearty hands clapped him on the back, those same hands extended for shaking between strikes and spares, he picked at his cheese fries, gone cold and rubbery from waiting and listening politely to congratulations, his wife and new baby there with him, his wife's faced creasing with worry whenever anyone said Iraq, so all the while he stared at his feet, the wall, the woman with the dark hair at the next lane, dodging the questions that came wrapped in good intentions, wrapped in praise and gratitude, but they came nonetheless, these nice people he swore to protect and serve, forever loyal, to the point of dying, they lobbed questions at him furiously, some he heard, some drowned out by Charlie Daniels on the jukebox, and still he threw ball after ball, his biceps burning as each question wound his arm further and further back—so what was it like over there? towel heads bad as they say? pins exploding up and back like bodies falling, and the asking started again when he came back from the lane, he mostly just nodded in answer, never really saying anything about the tedium of the camp, the heat, the goddamned heat and sand, the Diet Coke he hoarded, the 120 degree porta-johns, Iraqis watching Oprah, this surreal bit of home, that never overcame the worst sound of all—the crack-boom in the distance that meant an IED or mine went off, the hang-there for a moment of his heart hoping it was a near-miss rather than a direct hit, the fact that he heard that sound every day, the second worst sound of artillery firing without warning, because ours sounded just like theirs when the howitzers are that close, no matter how many pitchers of beer they buy him, he can't drown the day the battalion commander from 1st Battalion, 1st Marines handed him the dog tags of one of his Marines who had just been hit by a 60mm mortar, a great Marine, and how he was the one who brought the picture of the great dead Marine from where they'd hung it in the Intelligence Section back to his wife, he just wants to be here in a bowling alley in rural Virginia, near the little house where he grew up and near the lake where he lost his virginity and near the place where his daddy was buried, and he picks up a split, and everybody cheers at his deadly aim, and he nods and drinks and kisses his baby girl who coos in her seat now, safe and happy, and he ducks beneath the questions, lifting her to his chest, his scarred arms folding her in against him, and he smells soap and powder and the hint of the milk from his wife's young breasts, and he breathes in that smell, knowing he has ninety days, only eighty-nine now, before he's back in the middle of the night, on a dusty airfield, watching the better part of a battalion of Marines packed up and ready to go home after six months in al-Anbar, the relief etched in their young faces even in the moonlight, and as he files past loaded down with gear, he'll exchange a glance with a similar grunt, a Marine like him, going home, they'll say nothing. they'll ask nothing, nothing needing to be asked.

The Man at the Party

doesn't know that she doesn't hear him, just imagines his hands, tangled against her hair. Palms, then fists, she fits him where she needs, drawing on knowledge old as bone, she hones anatomical still-frames against the small talk, the scotch, and clatter of introductions, names she doesn't care to recall.

His hands are all she wants, the bulb of his thumb, to touch it with her tongue, giving in, licking words too ancient for sound into his palm. His hands are what she hears, despite the rules or ring he wears. When did we begin to care about

aidos? How vast the Greeks, seeking to bind honor with disgrace into a single word; chaste only defined by what is erotic. What evolutionary slip in the code made this knowingness true, ticked us past the curve of heat and lip, of joint and hip that already knew the holiness of coupling, sanctity of sex?

She chooses *aischune*, gray disgrace of having done. As he pours another drink, asks what she thinks of that famous name's last book, or the weather, she leans into a want older than shame, touches his hand as he passes the glass, sees only the primitive roll of his shoulders as she bends to prayer between his knees.

*aidos: from the Greek, shame that keeps one from doing; aischune: shame for something one has done

Galileo's fingers

turned up, finally, right thumb and middle finger, stolen from his corpse, from the basilica those three hundred years ago. A tooth, a bit of spine, too, hidden in a cup, blown glass and passed generation to generation of a marquis' family, passed like a birthright, like a surname, like titles and deeds to houses and walls, locked in a vault, only revealed in the whispers of death, until the whispers lost words, and no one even knew what the cup held anymore. When poverty bent the marquis' wild heirs, centuries into no longer noble, a collector of glass bid at auction and won the small cup, a vessel he bought for its crystalline globe, never knowing its gently curved bowl held the light touch of genius, the pulse of all time.

Showing Nightly

I had finally met the wrong person — and he was I. —Paul Mercurio

That place where time bent, where Everett spied the splintering of physics, the endless runs and corners, where the universe mocked, grinning like a curved chalice, that's where Jillian went to step into and out of her own body. She'd discovered the way one day when looking for her misplaced brown boot, the ones with the fuck-me heels, the ones she mainly wore on days that she felt the worst about herself and so consoled herself with slutty shoes and heavy blue eyeliner. The single boot had never reappeared. Instead, in the far left corner of her closet, there in the back where she only looked when something was lost, Jillian had seen a sliver of light that should not have been there. Electrical short, she thought at first, fear of fire near the top of her list of ways not to die, so she pummeled out the old boxes and bagged winter clothes, leaving them strewn about her room while she searched for the source of the light. And all the while, it grew, that light, from a sliver to a beam to a column rising to the top of the only closet in her cubicle of an apartment in its line of a million other cubicles. That first time, Jillian had knelt there on the closet floor, between a small box of wilted Christmas ornaments and the shimmer of a black sequined cocktail dress still with the Macy's tags, and hadn't looked, the light too bright, until she did look, and slid backward in surprise when she saw herself. Herself in China, walking the Great Wall. Herself in a boardroom, pitching, jewelry with bright blue stones falling like stars from her fingers. Herself wearing fur-lined boots and laughing in some stand of pine trees. Herself in confession, crying as she spoke. Herself stepping out of the sequined dress, in bed with a man with brown eyes. Herself kneeling alone on a closet floor. The light kaleidoscoped, breathed, opening and closing, while Jillian watched a thousand lives play out. All of them hers. So now each night, home from the insurance office, from days of filing other peoples' accidents and tragedies, she slips out of her heels, shuts the ringer on the phone, then carries a plate of beans or pasta, hastily heated, to the bedroom, where she kneels to watch, chewing slowly over what might have been.

Bestia Animus

Walking on the street in the dark, she turns to him, and he cries out that her eyes—her eyes shine like an animal's eyes, like an animal caught in passing beams, from a car or a flashlight. She laughs, a quick almost-not sound in the night—he's dreamed that sound—and tells him to look again, says look again as she lays long fingers on his arm, and of course, he sees nothing, nothing but calm and cool and pale pale blue. Ahead, the thick night thins, houses clump in groves, crouch beneath pooled light now of streetlamps, and she closes her eyes, he notices that she's closed her eyes, and thinks that she's closed them against the light, but that doesn't really put his mind to rest. It's a test, he thinks. From then on, the dialogue changes, from the night he saw phosphorescence or a vision of phosphorescence in her eyes, and now, he rearranges so he can leave a light burning, some lamp or fixture lit and burning, and raises a window, makes sure to raise a window, sometimes he opens them all, as a way to explain the jungle noise all around him, as a way to explain the shadows on the wall.

We All Need Those Forty Days

in the wilderness, at some point, given that this life is so locust-ridden, so plagued with the frogs of fear, the water so bitter with need. See what you can while you're there, learn the value of being lost, tossed in desert winds, scoured by sand until you can rediscover your own skin. Dig in, grasshopper fed, led where lonely becomes loved, where your soured feet stumble on to the music playing across half-buried bones, the bleached antelope, the auroch, bear and boar, lizard and leopard both crouching on those nearby rocks, waiting, watching you slack-jawed and wild. So you beetle back, slide to the stillness of the swamp's edge, to where Jeremiah and his stick struck the water sweet. Wade in, muck and spit beneath your blistered feet, Give in, step in, on day thirty-nine, under that sky relentless in its going on, only to find you and the quiet bittern both shy, both startled to learn, that you had the honey in your hands, all along.

It Is As One Body

for John Eaton

the heart breaks, and breaks, and lives by breaking. —Stanley Kunitz

it is as one body we inhabit the past, that body learned first and fast in hot snaky rows of a cornfield, some other day and year, gone before here, when a smooth-skinned boy with square fingers and almond eyes slid his hands from breast to belt, centuries she'd known him—felt blood and limb—but time folded their way home, time thinned and ridged and hollowed by song, knows better even than bone.

this body, its own history submissive even, made of bits trundled up from sand, all woman, all man, bending first into—then out, casting about, in search of itself, as whole--angled and sharp as the shade of long-leaf pine—what time knows is that it loves

hard lives, those field scarred, hearts lined with pitch, that boy gone man in broke-sole boots, that girl gone woman, cotton skirt hitched to hip, a crescent scar cupping there the womb—sharing its dichotomies, its shape with the heart.

listen! you have what you need—

time giving and heated, left for you, circled, handed over with ceremony that knowing, skin knowing—that the soul flees not out—

but in—

when it finds its own again.

The Real Politics of Lipstick

She learned the secret authority of her mouth at a young age, too young to form the words, but she understood the looks men gave at the innocence of the Tootsie Pop in her lips, a generous mouth her mother called it, easily sliding from a smile to a sulk, that ice cream cone a weapon that she wielded easily by the age of fourteen, the sweet cream of it deliberately left on the cushion of her bottom lip as she watched them stare, sweat, shift away from their wives. Look up at me, look up at me, they said, and she did, especially after she discovered the ultimate power of lipstick, blood red for regular guys her age, who wanted to rush, wanted to own the cleft of her upper lip, the tangle of hair they fisted at the crown of her head, but she switched to blushing pink for older men, that sweet slow youth they struggled to remember, cotton candy, candy apple smeared across her cheek as they mouthed thank you thank you thank. They all thought they were taking her, as she knelt, eyes lifted, thinking of nothing more than how for that moment, she owned them, branded each forever with the tip of her tongue, shadowy traces of lipstick that would never completely wash away.

Why She Keeps Leaving

You can't count a man happy until the day he dies. —Herodotus

That last man she fucked quoted Greek to the soft inner fold of her thigh, dialectic his life and the lie to his wife on the phone, his finger seeking and finding her clit. That old man she loathed quoted God, chapter and verse, among the anointed—*Get thee hence!*—he called her out, divining her fall, *porneuo, ekporneuo*, whore. That man she never loved quoted her, I do, she had said, white beaded vow, but didn't, and now, he asks how even as she drops his ring in a jar by the door. That dead man she loved quoted Auden by way of goodbye, the phone call just two tinny ticks from the forever-gone click of a trigger, while she slept, and slept.

We Buried the Arrows

near white roots, man, eagle, ox and lion, knowing that time would bend on itself again and again, three, ten, fifty thousand turns of the wheel, before the stories forced green shoots up through rocky soil. Some say cedar, its oily reach sweetened by the Tigris; some say white pine, needles in clusters of five, drinking deep from the river of saints, from Onadanga shores, and some say olive, named by prophets, *shajarat zaytun*, who sips from the deepest earth of all, so steady no drought will turn it bare. There, then, we called the rabbits from beneath the gooseberry, and the Syrian bear and the painted turtle and the fierce auroch gentled there in the shade of that great tree. We called the four winds, the four faces, and with Ezekiel, we nestled in the boughs, slept without dream in its shade. We sang the song that it made. We buried our sins, in soil now clay, now clay mixed with lime, farther on of sand, the surface rock soft limestone and basalt. We chewed figs and fried bread; with Jericho's salt, we boiled globes of thistle and made stew of nettle. The falcon, eagle, osprey and gull, even the gypsy wagtail, seeded beaks, lifted fruit to limb, first green then purple, coniferous, opening, slowly, so that we'd know. In the brush of their wings, the people, sharp-tipped Babylonian spear and sting of knapped stone, came home, buried our arrows and buried our dead, were sweetened and honed, opening like those cones. See them? There? Right there, pointed and fragrant as stars above our heads.

Sitting Naked in the Yard

should be required, where everything is watching you,
the shy-needled pine by the drive,
that crowd of crowfoot that's waiting,
sister plantain, the cedar and pin oak
shading your neighbor's yard.
The cardinals might turn their stately heads,
but not the neighbor's tabby, or the warblers,
the mockingbird and pristine jay, definitely
not the crabby woman with the garden gloves
who loves petunias and who already thinks
you think too much of yourself.
Show her, and the curious salamander
passing by, hot and brazen
on your naked thigh
what you got.
The only reason to live
is to give ourselves away.

Mary Carroll-Hackett earned an MFA from Bennington College and her work has appeared in numerous journals including *Carolina Quarterly, Clackamas Literary Review, Pedestal Magazine, Superstition Review, Drunken Boat* and *The Prose-Poem Project*, among others. She was a North Carolina Blumenthal Writer and winner of the Willamette Award for Fiction. Her chapbook, *The Real Politics of Lipstick*, won Slipstream's 2010 poetry competition, and another, *Animal Soul*, was released this year from Kattywompus Press. She founded and teaches in the Creative Writing programs at Longwood University. She also teaches workshops on Writing Grief and Loss, Writing the Body, Writing the Earth, and Writing through the Chakras at The Porches Writers Retreat in Virginia. Mary founded and edits *The Dos Passos Review, Briery Creek Press,* and *The Liam Rector First Book Prize for Poetry.* Most recently, she co-founded *SPACES*, an online magazine of art and literature. Mary is currently at work on a memoir.

www.ingramcontent.com/pod-product-compliance
Lightning Source LLC
Chambersburg PA
CBHW071740040426
42446CB00012B/2405